THE VALET MAN

THE VALET MAN

A TIME TO REMEMBER

Henry Valdez

The Valet Man

Copyright © 2023 by Henry Valdez. All rights reserved.

No part of this publication may be reproduced, stored in a retrieval system or transmitted in any way by any means, electronic, mechanical, photocopy, recording or otherwise without the prior permission of the author except as provided by USA copyright law.

The opinions expressed by the author are not necessarily those of URLink Print and Media.

1603 Capitol Ave., Suite 310 Cheyenne, Wyoming USA 82001
1-888-980-6523 | admin@urlinkpublishing.com

URLink Print and Media is committed to excellence in the publishing industry.

Book design copyright © 2023 by URLink Print and Media. All rights reserved.

Published in the United States of America
ISBN 978-1-68486-625-0 (Paperback)
ISBN 978-1-68486-570-3 (Digital)
20.09.23

Introduction

I have written several articles in my short time as a writer—sidelined by other careers, such as raising family of two children and four grandchildren. A twelve-year military career in the U.S. Navy helped establish my writing abilities as I studied many cultures and styles of literature. My marriage of fifty years gave me stories that you think only can happen to other families but not yours. Hope you enjoy some of them as we experience them through my eyes. Writing is something enjoyed by many, but only a few get to put them into words in a book.

My life as a VALETMAN showed me acts of kindness in so many ways, through people, in ways of verbal communication. The courtesy of opening the car door for the mother who has knee problems, getting the power chair from the trunk of a car for the grandmother, a wheel chair for the mother in labor due at any moment. A small act of kindness that would make a day trip to the hospital a bit easier to validate then having to be here at all. I was once told:" BE KIND= CAUSE YOU CANNOT REWIND" May you find the joy in your days, for you are the only one who can see it. Though my heart has yet to see the impact of writing, the joy it brings me never ends. I see it in the hearts it touches, the love it brings to write these stories.

Henry Valdez, VALETMAN

Contents

Retirement 9

He is Our Joy 11

How will I Know Love? 15

A Day at Work 19

Valeting is a Job! 23

A Day for Pets 25

Growing Up 29

A Time to Remember 31

Age is but a Number 35

The End of a New Beginning 37

My Window of Opportunity 41

The History of Valeting 43

Retirement

My retirement was fast and abrupt. After twenty-seven years at Automotive MFG in Georgetown, Kentucky, they announced that they were having a buy-out for those twenty-five years of service and fifty-five years of age. Quickly my mind started racing, I felt that quietness. Now, what are my other options? Pros and cons? How will it affect my finances? And most importantly, what will my wife think?

The MFG plant has been good to us in every aspect—financial, medical, entertainment, and social. Everything was sound and solid and now retirement. I adjusted my bills according to the buyout settlement. Social security will take care of my medical bills. A part time job will supplement my social life. I took it. My part-time jobs have been different and exciting so much that I wrote a book about my best job—VALETMAN, *an Act of Kindness*. Was it the right thing to do? It is still questionable. Given the situation at the time, my lower back and knees hurting all the time; arthritis on both arms and hands; and my age, I said no better time or alternative.

Five years later, I see no difference in my life. I changed certain habits; many are still a problem, but life remains the same. Children still want vacations as a family together, and in the end, the bills get paid. That's life as a retiree. Wow! Retirement is not measures in time spent working or accumulation of wealth, but in how your remaining time with family and friends are accomplished. You are given enough time to fulfill your every need with those you love, so enjoy every minute. That last laugh, that last picture, that last dinner by the ocean or mountain, savor that moment.

He is Our Joy

He ran into the field as if he knew what he was doing. It was his first day at soccer. Ten kids per team yet he managed to have eleven because they had the youngest boys off all of the other teams. Skylar would point to the positions he wanted the boys to stand at before the ball would be kicked, just as if he was the coach. Yet when the ball was kicked into play, all the boys would start running after it, except him. Hollering and screaming at all the kids to get him the ball, Skylar would only run if they got it close to him. As we would soon learn, like his dad, confrontation with others was not his best trait. He took to soccer only because his dad was the best soccer player in high school. The following year, he tried to play basketball. Tall for his age, he managed to keep up with the rest of the kids running up and down the court (without the ball). Skylar loved the yelling and screaming to the other kids to give him the ball, but once he got it, he wouldn't dribble the ball or pass it to the other kids. The referee would take the ball from him and put it back into play. As much as he liked playing basketball, he just didn't comprehend the concept of dribbling and scoring. Maybe he was still too young for this sport. Again we noticed that confrontation with other kids was a problem.

Now Skylar is seven and is a big boy as he keeps reminding us. Soccer season rolls around again, so his dad signed him up and decided to help coach the team this year. Dad has been working with him on his footwork and his confidence on scoring when the ball is near the net. Skylar tells us that there are too many kids around when he gets close to the net (confrontation). Anyway he knows what direction to go to to score points this time. It was a joy to watch him play this year, as he showed maturity and laughter in playing with others. For Skylar just turning toward us and waving after he scores and smiling when he kicks the ball out of bounds to keep the other team from scoring is a pleasure and joy to see and lasts us a lifetime. He is our big boy but will always be our baby forever.

The joy you bring us doesn't end I see you in the hearts you've touched, In all the things you love so much.

How will I Know Love?

I was eighteen years of age when I first realized what beautiful really was. My mom was beautiful so was my dog and cat. The way my mom talked to me with kind words and the way she would look at me first thing in the morning. Her face of joy and smiles that would be enjoying to just look at without making a sound. A lady of peace and pleasantries, knowing that this day was going to be a good day without worries and troubles. My mom's love was unconditional and forever. On the other hand, my dog and cat were just as cute and playful that you couldn't help but to pick them up and cuddle and squeeze them. They were as playful as they were warm and loving. Again *unconditional love forever*. Is this what real love is supposed to be?

In the next couple of years, I would learn to translate these feelings onto other people. My brother and sister were the first to receive my expression of what I would understand to be *sibling love*. My brother and I would make sure we would get to school or work on time. If something needed to be done or attended to, we would cover each other's back. If we weren't troubled or in trouble, we would address it and resolve it before it got too far out of hand. My sister was more of an *understanding love*. If she needed job support or work needed around the house, she would call me or I would ask. If it was financial, then we would work it out together. The understanding was always there; if she needed assistance in any way, shape, or form, I would be there for her. This was the love I grew up with. Did I know what *love* really was or the understanding of *love*?

On my twentieth birthday, my sister brought one of her closest friends to the house to do some homework she was having trouble with. I didn't see her arrive at the house, but I sure noticed her leaving that afternoon. The next day I asked my sister if I could call on her friend or maybe ask her out on a date. She said that she would ask, but no promises. Was this the *love* that I was looking for or just the infatuation that I was learning about at my age? I didn't know about infatuation at this point, as I have not been intimate with anybody else to achieve anything of such magnitude. Love has many interesting meanings or interpretations. Until you have lived life to its fullness, will one not truly understand what *love* is to oneself?When my first born was put into my arms, I did learn about a different kind of *love*. The feeling that went through me was a total blessing. Call it joy, fullness, or fulfillment of what God's blessing is all about. A *child's love* comes from the heart that you will give for the rest of your life, unconditional. No matter what they do or say, this is the one love that will never change. They come and go, three or four times in our lifetime, and we will forgive them and accept them because of who they are, not for what they are. As somebody before me once said, "They do no wrong." Every time you hug them, it feels like the first time when you held them in the hospital.

Now that I am married, with years of wisdom and the knowledge of caring, pretending, supporting, understanding and communicating, do all these things add up to *love* or is *love* a thing of its own with its own definition?

All this *love* installed in you from day one til the day you die from the one being who was with you always—God!

A Day at Work

My mornings seemed to all start the same. I get my desk in order by arranging my valet tickets one way and the binders another way. It seems that the night personnel have their own order of arrangements also. A couple of the night nurses say goodbye and a couple of the day shift nurses say hello! I watch the parking area fill up slowly, one-by-one; I can always tell how my day is going to be by the way the parking lot fills up. The young couples show up first, followed by the single moms and young grandmothers. Then the seniors come, and they are my best customers. They all seem to have their own personal reason for valeting their cars.

This particular morning was different from the beginning. I got go work fifteen minutes early because I have had a restless night, and I was waking up all times of the night. When I got to the hospital, the parking lot was three-fourths of the way full, which was very unusual. I had two cars, labor and delivery, waiting on me. By 6:30 in the morning, a third car pulled-up and parked a little past my valet station and stayed in the car. The tinted windows made it hard to see who was in it or how many people were in it also. By 6:45, I had three more cars pull up to valet. Now this seemed very unusual to be this busy this early. By 7:00 in the morning, my valet parking area was full. My day was going to be very busy and maybe prosperous as far as tipping goes. My normal customers started arriving by now, so I was having a very good day. At 7:30 my good friend Pam, who has bad knees, is handicapped and not in good health, had arrived. I usually parked her car by my valet station so she wouldn't have to do so much walking, but this time I was crowed on top. As I got into her car, I heard a popping sound, but I did not pay any attention to it as I was still too busy. Days like these are far and few in between, rarely does this happen, but I learned to appreciate them. Helping people is what makes this job worth doing.

THE VALET MAN

May you find the joy in your day, for you
are the only one who can see it.

Valeting is a Job!

These are the days we learn to appreciate. We start working as soon as we pull the podium outside, and it remains steady for the next hour or two. Today was very unusual because I managed to valet twelve cars in two hours, where it normally takes all day. I felt good about today, and since it had the makings off a prosperous (tips) day, I remain optimistic. I smiled at and thanked everybody, even if they didn't valet their car. *Pop! Pop!* I heard a loud sound, but I kept accepting every car that came up to my station. Everybody seemed to be extra nice to me also, telling me what a good job we were doing and how much it meant to them because of all the walking that was involved inside the hospital. I felt good myself, my knees weren't troubling me, my lower back felt better than it has in months.

I had time to think about the days when few people would even consider valeting their cars. Times were slow and not much money to be made. If a car pulled up near the podium, we knew it was to be deleted, no questions. People walking from the parking area would just stop and inquire about our valet service and would make promises that next time they would take advantage of our service. Sometimes they would just stop and talk about the weather in general. Some of the new valet personnel would be talking about the new cars they had driven during the week, but yet not one of them knew how to drive a 5-speed transmission stick shift. New hires would come and go like a carousel, so I didn't know how long they would last or how much information to teach them, as I was the training coordinator. Each new hire would be their own story as to why they took the job and why it meant so much to them. Then within a month or two, they, too, would be off to a new job.

The one thing I enjoy about valeting is the interesting people I get to meet— some old friends from high school to politicians and sports athletes.

A Day for Pets

I've been starting my days real slow when it comes to valeting cars. I am getting about one car an hour, when my normal is about five cars an hour. So now you know why I had time to discover my new friends.

I'll start with my early morning buddies—two wild ducks. I think they are male and female because they made a nest on top of the hospital building. Every morning, they announce their arrival by singing their way around the patio grassy area. I call it a loud noise, but I am certain to them it's their mating song or happy noise. They are a precious sight to see so early in the morning to start my day in the right direction.

Next, I hear my friends in the trees—two red birds and two sparrows trying to outdo each other in their chirping songs, letting everyone know that spring has arrived. *Happy as a lark,* as the saying goes. They sing and play with each other all day long, waiting for their eggs to hatch so they can teach their newborns how to fly and survive in their surroundings. The circle of life goes on with them, and they own the sky surroundings, at least in this area anyway.

Now, I found a new baby rabbit. I don't know where it came from or how it got here. It was hiding in the bushes and high grass. I saw it moving at first but paid no mind to it as it hopped around trying to keep it hidden from sight. It looked like just a baby from where I stood as it was very frightened. I told the groundkeeper as he brought a shoe box to catch him and take it home later. It was too cute to let it wander around with nowhere to go.

As I was retrieving what I thought was my last car, I noticed something crawling on the street. I stepped on the brakes so hard that I would have gone through the windshield if I had not had my seatbelt on. A large turtle was crawling around in our parking lot. I tried picking it up, but it would crawl back into its shell as if to tell me he was alright and to leave him alone. He seemed to know where he was going because there was a small stream ahead of him in the direction he was headed. I hurried him along, pushing him with my foot, so he would not be in danger of getting run over by a car.

Valeting is a rush and hurried business. The turtle could have gotten hurt on one of our regular busy days. Thank goodness!Now it's Friday, my last work day of the week. It's been a slow week so why not end it slower. I was coming back slower than usual from parking my first car at 8:30 in the morning.

I stepped onto the sidewalk, took about five steps, when a bullfrog landed from the sky right in front of me. Talk about being scared! My hair stood up around my neck and on my arms, sweat poured down my forehead. I believe I jumped so high that I touched the eight-foot ceiling above me! Wow! I don't know where he came from or even if he fell from the sky, but I beat him for the highest jump of the day!

So, next time I am having a slow week, just keep in mind all my friends that can make my day all but normal. Valeting cars can be hard and stressful, but the environment around gives us so much to be thankful for and to appreciate the small living things that can give us joy.

Back to work! I have three cars in line needing valeting!

God makes the plants and animals grow.

Growing Up

You never know when your childhood turns into manhood. My dad passed away when I was ten years old. I was the oldest of three siblings. It wasn't like I had to go to work or find a way to earn money. My duties and chores around the house changed. There was little to play outside, or watch cartoons, or play video games. That's when I grew up, not knowing, but a change in my lifestyle happened. There are other kids whose life does change at an older age into manhood, because they do have to live in the streets and earn money in any way possible. We are told that life is too short and enjoy it, but the truth is: We spend the first forty years establishing ourselves and the next forty years planning our retirement and how we are going to survive.

My life was different from day one. My parents never married. I was being tossed back and forth from mom to dad and dad to mom depending on who was working that week or weekend. First lesson I learned: My mom loves me a lot. I can do no wrong in her eyes. She's always holding and hugging me so tight that I have to pretend to cry so she will release me. Kisses…it's a wonder she has any lips left. She picks me up and kisses me; she puts me down and kisses me. She moves me somewhere, three more kisses. She tries talking that baby talk she does to me and she kisses me between words. Like I said, I can do no wrong with her.

My dad, on the other hand, only kisses me on the hellos and goodbyes. Lesson two: My dad is pretty straightforward and disciplinary. Two hours of TV, one hour of Fortnite, and four hours of studying or homework. I have to take my own bath and dress myself. Proper English spoken and "yes, sir" or "no, sir" must be addressed when spoken to. Very few things I can do on my own, otherwise I have to ask permission. It's hard, but I like it that way also.

Now with two parents, comes grandparents, wow! Four of them. I never knew what competition was until I met them. If I knew it would be this way all the time, I would have gone with the grandparents first and skipped the parents all together. They let me do anything, get anything at the stores, eat anything and stay up as long as I want. If one doesn't get it for me, the other set will. The grandpas hugged me and the grandmas kissed me, so that even works better for me. I love it! They take me to all the cool places that are always full of kids my age and older. They let me stay at different hotels for days and called it a vacation. I always got different toys and clothes that looked funny on me, but they thought it looked cute, so I didn't say anything. They let me play games on their cell phones and laptop computers, sometimes for hours on it before bedtime. They are always explaining things to me, like I could make a difference as to why they are what they are. They show me a lot of pictures and explain what they mean to me now or later in my life. But one thing they do show me and that's how to love and respect each other. Compromising in everything we say and do, not everything has to be my way. That's the most fun I have ever had, when I get to stay with my grandparents! Growing up is so much fun with them.

A Time to Remember

When we got to the water park, I told my grandma that I would be swimming in the shallow pool first. I noticed there were more girls than boys in the pool. 1 jumped in and went underwater a short distance until I bumped into a girl, of course. She smiled and said hello to me of all things, which blew my mind because I thought she would be mad. She was twelve years old, as I would soon learn. We played tag, along with her other two sisters, one was older and the other was younger. We played for a little while longer, when I decided to go to the children's Hot Tub. I didn't notice at the time but she followed me to the Hot Tub also, she pulled up from underwater and screamed "boo" at me as she sprang out of the water. Smiling at me and looking at me with those bright blue eyes, I hollered out loud and quickly asked her what she was doing over here. She said she wanted to hang out with me and play around. That seemed nice of her, as I didn't have anybody else to play with. After the hot tub we went to the giant slide that I have never been on before, but I wasn't going to show my fear. We went side by side on different slides, and I was screaming, hoping she would not hear me. Half way down, I heard my name being hollered, so when we got done, I asked her if that was her that hollered my name and she said yes. She said she heard a lot of screaming and she wanted to know if I was alright. I asked her how she knew my name. She said she heard my Papaw called me for something. So I asked her what her name was. She said it was Madison, and I remember smiling real big for some reason because she asked me if it sounded funny to me. I said no quickly and that I thought it was a pretty name. From there, we went on the Lillypods Crossing. We both tried it, but we fell off coming out of the water laughing so loud not knowing what about. Next we went to the Lazy River on tubes. I got her tube first not knowing what to expect from her. She took off running in the water with the tube, so I chased her in mine. She screamed back at me, "First one to go around is the winner." I always like the challenges because my Mamaw would always say we would smell like rotten eggs if we were to lose, and I didn't want to smell like that to Madison (as I remember her name). I caught up to her about halfway through the stream but then she took off and beat me. We smiled again as we were having so much fun that we forgot what time it was. We had been playing for three hours when my Papaw hollered at me that it was time to eat lunch. Papaw said we were having McDonald's hamburger and that we had plenty if my friend wanted to eat with us. About that time, her dad showed up also and told her that it was time to eat. We both went our separate ways and told each other that we would meet up after we ate at the same spot in an hour. My Papaw asked me if I was having fun. I said yes and this was the best park ever! After eating lunch, my dad asked me if I wanted to go to the arcade and play games. I said yes real fast and jumped from my chair heading toward the arcade room. My dad loves the games as much as I did because he made them fun and always made me laugh. As we were playing, I remembered that I was supposed to meet Madison at the Lazy River after we ate. I was having so much fun with dad and Papaw that time went by so fast. I begin thinking about all the fun I had with Madison that I wanted to be with her again. I hope she wasn't mad at me or didn't want to talk to me anymore.

It was 7:00 at night already, so Mamaw and Papaw took me to the front of the park to see the Wolf Lodge Animal play made just for kids. It was fun, but I still was thinking about Madison, what was she doing and if she was even watching the play like I was. I wanted so bad to see her just to say hi. It was getting late, and we were heading back to our room when I heard somebody called out my name. As I turned my head toward the stairs above us, I saw her. I said hi! With a big smile and motion for her to wait for me. My Papaw took me upstairs where we sat and talked. I told her how much fun I had with her but that we were leaving in the morning. She said she was sad but that she had fun with me also. As we walked away, I grabbed my Papaw's hand and I asked him if we could come back again, and he assured me we would. My Mamaw said I went to bed with a big smile on my face that night, so she knew I had a good time at Great Wolf Lodge that day.

I will never forget how much fun I had with Madison, if only for that short moment of time we spent. A time in my life I hope to always remember. I was only seven years old.

HENRY VALDEZ

Be kind; can't rewind.

Age is but a Number

Age tells us how long we have been on earth. It measures the time we are joined with our family. We passed on the past, the present, and the future of what our world has been like. We can tell you what our children were like and how they grew up to make us proud, and their children growing up in comparison to them. We live through the good times in life and how we managed to get through the bad times with our experience and knowledge of times. But the one thing that we cannot talk about is our health and body. Does our body fail us or do we fail it? Do we exercise enough or do we eat all the right food needed for our nourishment? Is working out three days a week better than five days a week? Is drinking that protein drink better than a full course breakfast? We will do anything to keep our bodies strong and perform the necessary activities to get us through our daily life routines. Age is but a number, but our bodies are measured by our lifestyle and wear and tear of our daily performances.

I worked for twenty-seven years on an assembly line, concrete walking, standing face-to-face processes, ten hours a day, five days a week. I would do all the necessary chores needed around the house and would find enjoyment in my time left after all the necessary things were completed. My work was my exercise, and I would try to eat the right things or what my wife would fix when I got home. I was successful on both counts when measuring my life longevity.

My wife was successful on both counts but with different results. She managed to work for thirty-three years on her job. She also endured the walking on concrete everyday and standing on her feet for eight hours a day. Lifting heavy boxes and cooking and preparing nutritious meals everyday for three or four kids. She did not endure the positive finish at her job that I did. Even though she is three years younger than me and worked five years longer than I did, her final results were completely opposite of mine. Your body ages at a different rate than your age.

She was born a strong and healthy baby (6lbs 9oz size). Beautiful, smart, and attentive…you know she was destined for a good and prosperous life. A solid background and religious upbringing… you just knew she was going to go far in life. Her education was solid, good schools and good grades to match. She was going to go far in life that the only thing that could stop her was her health. She enjoyed every aspect of her life. She was numerous and fun to be around. She took her jobs and her work very seriously. Her marriage was shaky, but she stood her ground and made it work for fifty plus years.

She retired not because of her years of service but because of her health. Her knees were so bad that she would require knee surgery on both knees, although not at the same time. Walking was so bad that she could no longer do steps. A trip to the store was almost impossible. I would have to take a short grocery list as I could not carry a lot of bags by myself, since I was developing lower backache and would limit my distance when carrying heavy items. Without your health, age is but a number anymore.

The End of a New Beginning

I got in my first car and drove it to the valet parking lot like I owned it. I thought about valeting cars for the rest of my retirement life. This was too easy. Parking cars and retrieving them seem like a job I could do with no need of assistance and as long as my health stayed in check, no telling how long I could hold out. The pay was not great, but the exercise was just what the doctor ordered. My first year went by so fast that I failed to realize that my anniversary date had come and gone without a hitch. My second year started a little tough. A twisted ankle is something I never thought could happen to me. My legs and feet were the strongest part of my body that I never imagined them giving way to a small injury that would impact me for years to come. Still, I managed to survive the second year. Now in my third year, I was moved from the front to the rear side of the hospital of the hospital because it was at a slower, easier pace. I sometimes think this was a good move for me as this is when I got the idea of writing my book. This backside of the hospital was a whole different world that nobody would ever imagined even existed. Newborn babies, mothers of all ages, and colonoscopy stories that people would talk about would make you think what is really going on in the ER room under anesthetic! This was a good move for me. The first three years was all new for me, as

I never had to work outside during the winter and the driving of all different vehicles made my life a fantasy world. New cars, old cars, small ones, and large trucks. Push buttons, keyless entries and, yes, even the 5-speed transmissions still in existence. Little did I know that my new beginning to my new career was coming to an end. The signs were there for me to see and the changes were obvious.

It was the beginning of my fourth year, when I got back from my two-month playoff. I always takes two months off during the winter as it as getting harder to stand the cold days outdoor for me. First sign: I was told that we had double the number of cars being valeted at my station. We would need to work two persons, compared to before it only took one. End sign: We doubled the traffic; that meant I had to walk or run twice as much, which wasn't good for me. My feet were really hurting by this time. I had cut back on the running by this time and was just doing what I called, my fast-walking stride. Third sign: The newness and excitement that had carried me through the years had started to wear down on me; now I was just starting to survive. People started to seem more cranky and unappreciative of my services, or so it appeared. Was I doing something different? Was it me that was changing? I was past my prime, and my golden years were starting to show. After all, I did manage to reach my seventy years of age due to my wife's good cooking and tender loving care, as they used to call it.My fifth year was going to be my best year yet! My health was good, and my feet did not hurt. For the first time, my wife said I could keep my paycheck and use it for whatever I see fit. We have never been in that position before, so the first thing I did was but me some new shoes. What a magnificent way to start a new year!

THE VALET MAN

If I had any idea what this year had in store for me, I would never have come back.

First, let me start with the easy parts: Both my feet began to hurt. My work car of nineteen years, a 2000 Chevy Malibu, would not start on a couple of occasions. I've never had problems from this car as I took good care of it and had done maintenance checks on it on scheduled times accordingly. Then on my yearly doctor visit, I was told that I had low scores on some of my important vitals. If one would look at me, one would think, why does he even need to see a family physician? Why? To make matters worse, complaints started to appear on me. I was being rude to my customers; I was taking too long to retrieve cars, too slow on accepting cars, and causing a traffic jam at the entrance way to labor and delivery area. By mid-year, I committed the number one offense that we valet people never want to do and that is scratch or wreck a customer's car. I managed to do both in one week. Now leading to the end of August, I was at my lowest point ever. Feeling very distraught, I knew I had to make a major decision about my job. Is this the end to a once enjoying and best job a retired man could ever have? Was this the end? I told my wife that since the enjoyment of my job was gone, I could not do it any longer.

I started on the fifth day of October; I would quit on that same day. My new beginning had come and now gone so quickly that I did not have time to look back and enjoy the accomplishments. There are no regrets as I had been blessed to have done what I did for that many years. Now I must move on as one door closes another might and perhaps will open for me. I am looking!

My Window of Opportunity

I got to my assigned Plaza 3 door early, just in case I have some early customers waiting for my valet services. I look around at my surroundings just to see if I have notice anything has changed from the previous day.

Two things about my window that I look out every morning are:
1. I stay warm inside during cold days;
2. I can see everyone coming and going in the driving area.

It's good when they are leaving, which means there will be some vacant spots in the parking lot available for those early customers. This will make my job a little bit easier. As I look out the window again, I can clearly see the ambulance area beginning to become a very busy place. One would never think that the more activity in this area, the more customers it brings over to us. The families following these ambulances need to get inside very quickly, so they think of valeting as a quick and easy alternative to parking themselves.

My window of opportunity just got brighter as the road leading up to my valet station is very clear as I can see at least ten cars leading my way. Of those ten cars, five will park themselves, three will need valeting, and the other two will be undecided. The weather has a lot to say whether I will have a heavy busy day or a cold and slow day instead. Cold weather has a tendency to bring more customers to us. So as I look out the window, I am trying to figure out what kind of day this will be.

I can see the birds flying around aimlessly, looking for a nesting place. The wild geese returning to their last year's nesting ground to begin their new family for the coming months. The buds on the trees and bushes are telling me that spring is near and coming. Out of my window again, it shows me in no uncertain terms that the beauty will spring upon us is coming.

I can only hope for the best and help those in need.

Some have mirrors of images.

Some have mirrors on walls that tell where they might fall.

Others have a looking glass that tell the future.

But, my glass of opportunity tells me all of what lies ahead for me.

The History of Valeting

The history of valeting can only be measured by the experience of one's own personality. The work ethics one person puts into the job and changes a person goes through in years' time, makes that history.

Valeting cars has always been described to me as parking a car in a designated area marked *For Valet Only* and retrieving cars from that area and returning it to it's original pick-up spot; it's that simple. This could not be more wrong than anything ever told to any new employee ever hired. Courtesy and attitude are the first thing that head the list. When a car first arrives, you have to show that you will take care of their car in the words you speak in greeting them. Then the trust that you will take care of that car in the confidence that you know how to start and drive the car.

I mention starting a car because of the many variations of where the start buttons is located and where the keys go to start their car. Positive attitude also is key to valeting. People come to the hospital expecting bad news and a hard time finding a parking spot as we are currently going under a construction phase in the parking garage. So the more assistance and help we can provide, the better they feel.

Valeting has been around a long time. If there is a large parking lot, there will be valet services. It started with the hotel business first then expanded to the hospital districts of which I am associated with. I describe it as two different animals but with the same skin.

Valeting used to be for the young students and college kids but as better paying jobs entered the work force, they started leaving. That's where I came in, the retired workforce, more dependable and not worried about the pay scale.

Courtesy and respect are the main two reasons that our age group works so well. After five years of service, which is long in today's time, I have gained a lot of knowledge and experience of which I am able to tell my story, my history of valeting as seen through my eyes—the thrills and excitements, the sadness and disappointments as only I have seen.

This makes my retirement more enjoyable and exciting!

www.ingramcontent.com/pod-product-compliance
Lightning Source LLC
LaVergne TN
LVHW021741060526
838200LV00052B/3412